SuCCCess in Fund-Raising is Spelled with 3 C's

CONTACT
CULTIVATE
CLOSE

by Jerry F. Smith, CFRE

Be the Best!
Jerry Smith

Other Books by Jerry F. Smith, CFRE

*Fund-Raising: Rules of the Road to Success, featured in
the Library of Congress*

*Cultivating and Sustaining an Annual Fund in
Your Christian School*

For their hard work and dedication to this project, I would like to thank Megan Augustine and Elaine Jimmerson. Without their assistance, this book would not be in your hands today.

I also want to give a special thanks to the following individuals who have given of their time and talents to help me succeed in my life and business ... Buck Bradberry, Roger Schifferli, Bill Shelnutt, Wayne Smith and Buddy Weaver.

TABLE OF CONTENTS

People ask me all the time, "How long have you been in fund-raising?" Instead of replying in years, which makes me sound old, I used my calculator to figure up that I have been in this business 12,000 days. So, now when people ask me how long I have been in the business, I can tell them.

When I look back on my 12,000 days in this business to see what I have really learned, several things emerge. First, I am impressed with what a great profession fund-raising is to be in. However, I have learned from talking to development professionals who have worked in fund-raising for a few months, or even a few years, that they really don't know what they are supposed to do. There is little mentoring in this business. While I have benefited from a mentoring relationship with a retired development consultant, most of what I've learned has been from the school of hard knocks and experience. I've made more mistakes than anybody in this business, but I have used my mistakes to improve. How can I get better? How could I have done that differently? Realizing you will make mistakes and learning from them will help you move ahead and get better in the business of fund-raising. That's why I wrote this book.

American jazz, country and blues guitarist and songwriter Les Paul passed away in 2009 when he was 94. He performed in New York City every Monday at a small club called the Iridium Jazz Club. When my travels took me to NYC on Mondays, I always tried to see Les Paul perform. For the younger generation, Les Paul was a living legend. He was an outstanding performer with several number one hits. But he was equally important in creating the electric guitar and inventing some of the most basic sounds that recording artists and music fans now take for granted. In 1948, he shattered his right arm and elbow in a car accident. Undeterred, he had his surgeons set his arm at an angle that would allow him to cradle and pick the guitar. When asked later in life about his long career and influence, he said, "I don't think I'm very successful; I just constantly try to improve." When I read this comment, I was so moved, because here was a man who accomplished so much, yet he never thought he had arrived. He was always trying to get better. Wow, what an attitude! As fund-raisers, we should constantly try to improve. We are all on a journey not a destination. Learning takes place at every curve of the road. Without a doubt we will all make mistakes, but if we can learn from those mistakes, then we can say at the end of our careers, "I just constantly tried to improve!"

The second thing I've learned in 12,000 days on the job is that the following formula is a good tool for guiding development officers:

$$(BP + CS)E = Success$$

That is, (Basic Principles + Common Sense) x Effort = Success

Development requires a lot of all three. You have to utilize the basic principles of fund-raising, use your God-given common sense to guide you, and be on the road seeing people and building relationships. It's all about relationship-based fund-raising.

Thirdly, I've learned that there is no shortage of money, only a shortage of big, bold, exciting ideas. There are people out there who are willing to change the world and make those six and seven-figure contributions to an organization. It is your duty to show them how they can get involved and make a difference with a gift. According to *Giving USA*, in 2012 the American public gave away nearly $300 billion to non-profit organizations. Everybody has their hand out. Everybody's looking for that charitable dollar. What do you have to do? You have to make your organization a priority with your constituency. It's up to you as the development officer to ensure your constituency knows that you're a good organization and a good steward of the money they are contributing.

One thing I always point out when talking about how much money is given away annually in America is that 70-75% of the money is donated by living individuals. What does that tell you? It tells you about your constituency. If you're going to try to raise money, you need to think about how you're going to raise money from the <u>individuals</u> who are closely associated with your organization. Again, it's relationship-based fund-raising.

Finally, I've learned that fund-raising is both an art and a science. The science side deals with tangibles like numbers, analyses, projections and proposals. The intangibles are the art; things like personality, friendship, courtesy, relationships, strategy, respect, persistence and gratitude. The best fund-raisers I know are the ones who have a heart for the organization's mission, can communicate the passion and vision of the organization both verbally and in written form, pay attention to the myriad details of development work, and have a strong work ethic. If you have those characteristics, you can learn to be an excellent fund-raiser.

It's a relationship business, and it is with regard to people that we must learn to CONTACT, CULTIVATE and CLOSE in order to be suCCCessful.

CONTACT

CHAPTER ONE

CONTACT OR SIGHTING?

Think about the number of individuals you run into on a weekly basis---at church, at work, in the mall, in the grocery store, at your child's soccer game, at an event or a football game. Those meetings have a role in fund-raising, but they are not what I call a contact. Instead, I call those "chance" encounters or sightings. (I put "chance" in quotation marks because I don't believe in random events. Rather, I believe even unplanned, brief meetings are divine encounters and should be treated as such.)

Why are sightings important? Because they contribute to your public persona. Your courteousness, your friendliness, your kindness toward every person you meet can turn into an asset in fund-raising. A chance encounter often leads to an actual fund-raising contact.

I was onsite at a school recently. When the president of the school and I came back from lunch, we pulled into a parking spot next to a Lexus SC430. Now, a Lexus SC430 is a hardtop convertible and costs about $70,000. The woman sitting in the driver's seat had the windows down. It was a warm day, and I leaned over on the passenger side and said, "Excuse me. How do you like your car?" She replied that it was a great car. Then I asked if she had a child at the school, which she did, and I asked her name. We talked a few more seconds before the president and I walked toward the school entrance. It turns out, the president didn't know the woman. (If I had known that, I would have introduced them!) We went straight to the director of development to tell her the woman's name. She did a quick online search of the name, found out the husband was in construction, and through electronic screening, we discovered the family was capable of making an annual gift of $50,000 to $100,000. That's a contact.

So, what's the difference between a sighting and a contact? See if you can find the key element that defines a contact from this definition:

A contact is an individual, company or foundation that has been *pre-qualified* as a prospective donor.

That's right---*pre-qualified* is the operative term. Pre-qualified means you have established the relationship of the contact to the organization and have done research on what this contact is capable of giving.

How do you identify those individuals, companies and foundations? One thing I like to tell development officers and educational institutions is to take part in our "car duty," like in the example above. When parents drop their children off in the morning, you should be out front welcoming the students. Why? You will find out who's driving the expensive cars---Lexus, Mercedes, Cadillac, etc. This will help build your list of potential contacts.

One development officer told me recently that he knew of three families in the elementary school that dropped their children off in two Bentleys and a Rolls Royce. Do you think they would be prospects? Yes, of course.

Be observant of your prospects. What do they drive, what do they wear, where do they live, what kind of watch do they wear? Look them up on the web; there's lots of information out there.

1. *The names in your portfolio of prospective donors should be pre-qualified.*

2. *Spend your time building relationships with pre-qualified contacts.*

Philippians 2:5 "In your relationships with one another, have the same mindset as Christ Jesus."

CHAPTER TWO

MINING FOR DONORS

All potential donors are important, but you do not have time to see them all. You will wisely learn to spend time cultivating those pre-qualified donors who are capable of making leadership gifts to the organization. Former Auburn University head football coach Pat Dye once told me that he only had 24 hours in each day; he had to spend that time with individuals who could help Auburn University and the football program. This is not to discount the smaller gifts that might come from your prospect pool, but those funds might be solicited a different way---perhaps a direct mail appeal followed by a phone call. Keep in mind that 90% of your money comes from 10% of the donors, so you need to determine who those donors are and spend time cultivating and soliciting them to be successful.

For the purposes of this discussion, a contact is someone with whom we can have a meeting of substance that we have pre-qualified as being capable of making a significant gift toward the project.

There is a four step process to pre-qualify potential donors: Electronic Screening, RFM Analysis, Inclination Ratings and Committee Verification.

1. **Electronic Screening and Data Mining Services**: By using electronic screening, you are able to take a large data base of names and, without using Social Security numbers, prioritize a data base. In other words, the screening can help you find the needle in the haystack. I suggest that development officers carry a portfolio of 150-200 prospects, or contacts, with whom they are working. Electronic screening is a way to effectively sort a large data base into manageable blocks, based on giving potential. Here's an example of the type of information electronic screening can provide:

A small private school with whom we worked on one occasion furnished us a list of 423 names of potential donors---not pre-qualified, but potential. The electronic screening service used 19 different parameters to examine this list and returned to us the following information:

- The total giving capacity for the names was $22,742,735.

- One person had the capacity to give between $1 million and $5 million.

- Five people could give between $500,000 and $1 million.

- Nine people could give between $250,000 and $500,000.

- 30 people could give between $100,000 and $250,000.

- 43 people could give between $50,000 and $100,000.

- 157 people could give between $25,000 and $50,000.

- The balance of the list would be able to give less than $25,000.

This told us that there was significant giving capacity at the school. The electronic screening service returned to us a list of names with their giving capacity. However, this information does not tell us the following: an individual's net worth or their inclination to give to your organization. It only tells us their capacity to give to any organization. It is the job of the fund-raiser or development officer, through one or more contacts, to discover inclination and ultimately bring inclination up to the level of capacity.

2. **RFM Analysis:** An RFM analysis is a three-part score used to help institutions identify the best prospects from all current donors. The score combines measurable factors such as recency (R), frequency (F) and monetary (M) giving. The recency component rewards donors whose last gift was received within the last five years. The frequency score rewards donors who give, and give often over time. Monetary scores reward donors who have

made large outright gifts and have given a significant amount over time. Each score is weighted to place a degree of emphasis on that component as follows: R=20%, F=30%, M=50%. In order to perform an RFM analysis, six data elements must be present: first gift date, last gift date, cumulative giving total, single one-time giving total, single one-time largest gift, and total # of gifts. It is important to note this methodology cannot rank any constituent who has no giving history with an organization.

The Recency score applies anywhere from 0-20 points to a prospect based upon the date of the last gift made to the institution in question. Any gift made within the last calendar year (365 days), receives the maximum score of 20 points. Each subsequent year receives five points less, with any donor whose last gift was over five years ago receiving no points.

- Gifts within the last 365 days, 20 points

- Gifts within the last 730 days, 15 points

- Gifts five years old (1,461 – 1,825 days), 1 point

- Gifts over five years, no points

The Frequency score is a two part score. The first part divides the total number of gifts a donor has made to the organization by the total number of years of giving. The second part is a multiplier that rewards donors who have a history of giving over many years. A donor who has made multiple gifts over three years would not receive as high a score as a donor who has made a significant number of gifts over a longer time span, say 10 years for example.

The Monetary score also has two components. The first part of the score assigns up to 25 points based on the cumulative dollars given. The second part of the score assigns up to an additional 25 points based on the size of the single-largest, one-time gift made. If an institution has certain recognized giving levels, those would be good breakdowns to use when setting up the point scale; however, it can and should be modified if necessary to create separation. One does not want everyone to score highly because the top categories are made too achievable.

One of the benefits of this ranking system is that the point ranges can be modified for individual clients to help create separation throughout their donor database. By identifying those prospects who have an affinity and willingness to make significant donations on a regular basis, there is a better chance of measuring prospective campaign potential. This also helps to minimize bias recent donors may receive due to the "freshness" of their gifts. Finally, it helps to bring donors into the mix who may not be the usual suspects an institution relies on time and again. Unsolicited donations may go relatively unnoticed when compared to solicited donations that involve personal interactions and relationship building. The RFM methodology helps to remove personal elements from the equation and bring a more scientific approach to the process.

3. **Inclination Ratings:** After receiving the electronic screening of your records, and applying the RFM analysis, the next step is assigning inclination ratings to determine what the prospect's capability is to make a gift to *your* organization or constituency. Remember, electronic screening does not tell you an individual's net worth or inclination to give---only the capacity to give. You have to determine what capability they have to give to *your* organization. RFM analysis yields the data to determine their inclination to give to your organization.

Prospects are ranked on a scale of 1 to 5, with 1 being low inclination and 5 being high inclination based on their relationship with your organization as defined by their total RFM score. In addition to the metrics used to determine the RFM score, you may add additional or "bonus" point values based on their participation on boards or volunteer groups, attendance at events, etc. You assign a level of importance to each metric based on its importance to your organization.

The maximum achievable score for the RFM is 100. Determine the level of importance and assign a point value for your "bonus" participation points and add them to the RFM score. For example: You may have five bonus points for a Giving Society or Advisory Board Member, 10 bonus points for a Board or Campaign Steering Committee Member, and 15 points for the Chair of a Board or Campaign Steering Committee.

Examine your total RFM (RFM + Bonus Points) and look for breaks or separations in the numbers. The data for each screening will break out differently. Remember, the inclination rating is a scale of 1 to 5, with 1 being low inclination and 5 being high inclination. For example: Anyone with a total RFM of 90 or more may be assigned an inclination rating of 5; anyone with a 70 to 89 total RFM may be assigned a 4; a total RFM of 55 to 69 may be a 3; a total RFM of 40 to 54 may be a 2; and anyone below a 40 may be a 1. The RFM point break determining the inclination ratings will be different for each organization and for each screening for the same organization. The data must always be examined with each screening to determine the ranges for inclination ratings.

Next, you assign the unqualified ask amount. The unqualified ask amount is based on the electronic screening capability and the inclination rating. The inclination rating is assigned a definite percent value. An inclination rating of 1 is assigned a percent value of 10%, 2 is 20%, 3 is 30%, 4 is 40% and 5 is 50%. Multiply the inclination rating percent value by the electronic screening capability. For example, if the electronic screening says a prospect is capable of making a $100,000 gift, and you have determined their inclination rating to be 1, you multiply $100,000 by 10% to yield an unqualified ask amount of $10,000 for your organization.

4. **Committee Verification:** A prospect verification committee is a group of six to 10 individuals affiliated with and committed to your organization. Perhaps they are leaders of the organization, long-time members and/or supporters, members of good standing in the community, etc. They comprise a group that has a more-thorough-than-normal knowledge of the organization's potential donors.

The prime responsibility of this committee is to review pre-established ask amounts from the electronic screening, RFM analysis and inclination rating processes. They verify the ask amount or suggest a higher or lower ask amount based on personal information or knowledge of the individual. Members of the committee will likely know about life situations of those on your top prospect list (those with an inclination rating of 3 or higher). For example: Someone who has been out of work for six months; someone who is undergoing major medical expenses; someone who is planning on moving out of town and will lose contact with the project; someone who has just come into an inheritance or other financial windfall; and the general economic level of almost everyone on the list.

These life situations may greatly impact an individual's or family's capacity to give. A committee of knowledgeable individuals can do an excellent job of verifying an individual's capacity to give once they pool their knowledge. When capability levels are verified by the committee, contact can be scheduled accordingly, giving priority to those with the highest capability.

Verifying prospects requires soft information as well as hard data. Electronic screening can yield false or misleading information because of duplicate names that are not your prospect and changes in the financial market. As soon as the screening is complete, it's old. Financial markets and people's wealth is constantly changing. Electronic screening, RFM analysis and inclination rating assignment is just a snapshot. Committee verification can assist with determining a more accurate picture of your prospects' capacities to give.

My experience with this system is that it shows remarkable accuracy in developing an ask amount that is in keeping with the donor's capability and propensity to give. Why? Because through electronic screening, you learn of capability you previously had no knowledge of, and through human evaluation, that information can be run through the grid of real life situations. One of the biggest mistakes in fund-raising is not asking for a specific dollar amount. Gathering this information is a must for your success in fund-raising.

If you gather this information, you have to manage it. The development office is primarily responsible for managing and protecting this information—it must be kept confidential and managed with the utmost integrity. The development officer gathers the information from volunteers, the president, the board and other development staff and ensures that it is entered accurately into the organization's database. The more information you have, the better you will know your prospects, and the more successful you will be in asking the right person, at the right time, for the right project and the right dollar amount.

Regardless of how you do it, pre-qualifying and verifying your prospects is absolutely critical to the fund-raising efforts of any organization for two reasons: time is limited and energy is limited. Pre-qualification prioritizes your time and energy so you focus on contacts with the capability of making a major gift to your program. It also allows you to assign prospects to your development officers with some expectation of the contact's ability to give.

Once you are assigned 150 to 200 prospects with potential ask amounts, how do you prioritize the list? You begin by sorting the list by the qualified or verified ask amounts. Then sort by the inclination ratings within the high dollar amounts. Work on the 5s first, then the 4s, then the 3s, etc. The inclination level assigned to each prospect is the key. Why? Because they may not have the highest dollar capability, but they have the highest gift capability and the highest relationship level.

Is this individual only somewhat interested in the organization? Is their name in the data base merely because they signed up for a raffle two years ago? I'm looking for involvement. It's a basic principle in our business that people who are involved in organizations tend to become committed to those organizations and the dollars follow the commitment. If you identify top prospects who are not involved, get them involved before you make the ask. The single most important reason people make gifts to charitable organizations is because they are involved.

We once did a feasibility study for a school in Florida. I said, "Who do you feel is your biggest prospect here?" They told me, and I said, "What is his involvement?" They said, "Well, he's not really involved. His wife is involved, but he's not involved." In the course of our conversation, they mentioned doing a strategic plan. I said, "Why don't you ask him to chair this strategic planning process?" They did ask him, and he agreed. It was a three-month process, and he got very involved in the school during that time. When they started their campaign, we were hired to manage it. The first thing we did was ask him if he would chair the campaign; then we asked him if he would consider a gift of $250,000. In both instances, he said yes. Again, I think had he not been involved, he probably would not have agreed to either of our requests. Don't ever lose sight of the importance of involvement.

You need leadership gifts. Start with individuals first. Consistent givers, even if it is only $5 a year, are committed to your organization---they are top prospects if they have leadership capability. Corporations only give away 5% a year, and foundations have hundreds in line in front of you that want their dollars. Individuals should be your first priority. Your best prospects for leadership gifts are those with high capability *and* high inclination levels.

Now you are ready to establish contact with the prospective donor.

1. *Consider using electronic screening, especially if your data base is large.*

2. *Use both objective and subjective information in determining the right ask amount.*

"By failing to prepare you are preparing to fail."

Benjamin Franklin

CHAPTER THREE

SETTING THE APPOINTMENT

Setting the appointment is the most important and the hardest part of any solicitation or cultivation meeting. Once an appointment is secured, 80% of the work is done. The best way to get the appointment is to show a genuine interest in the prospect you are calling and your support of your organization and its mission. If you support and believe in the mission, they are more likely to support and believe in it as well. A sincere, enthusiastic attitude by you about the organization and its campaign or project will excite and motivate the prospect to give serious consideration to your request for an appointment.

Before you begin, you must be organized. Compile your list of names with top prospects first. The top prospects are the key appointments. Make phone calls three to four weeks before the trip to allow plenty of time for scheduling. Make a list of available appointment days and times before you begin calling, and allow 30 to 40 minutes for each meeting. Avoid lunch or breakfast meetings whenever possible. Unnecessary interruptions in a public restaurant can make discussions awkward. Research your prospects before you call.

When you begin calling, remember to be politely assertive and always be yourself. Be prepared to offer several potential appointment times. Offer an available slot, but be ready with several other dates and times in order to find something convenient for the prospect. Always indicate the number of people coming and who they are. If you are cultivating a couple, always schedule the appointment with both of them if possible. This avoids the inevitable, "I'll have to talk to my spouse and get back to you." However, if only one person is available to meet, schedule the appointment.

If you have a cell phone number, begin with it and move to the office and home number if you are unable to reach them on their cell. One of our university clients is having great success with sending appointment requests through email blasts to a large number of prospects for initial visits. This is done through a mail merge in Microsoft Word so that the email looks as if it was sent to each recipient individually addressing them personally. They are receiving a 10% response rate and half of those are scheduling appointments. Here's an example of an e-blast sent out by the development coordinator on behalf of the development officer:

<Salutation> <Last Name> ,

Jon Smith, who works for Dean Bob Jones in the College of Engineering here at XYZ, will be in the Virginia/DC area October 16-18, 2012. The purpose for visiting, on behalf of the Dean, is to reconnect with XYZ Engineering Alumnus and update them on Dean Jones' vision for the College of Engineering.

Jon has asked that I contact you to see if you would have some time to meet with him during his trip. Please let me know which day and time work best for you.

Best regards!

Development Coordinator

Your Signature Information Here

For this particular e-blast, 158 emails were sent in 10 minutes. Within three hours, there were 15 responses and seven appointments set. Within two days, there were 33 responses and 14 appointments set.

Keep accurate records of whom you contact and their response, confirm the appointment location, and take detailed notes of information they share.

Prospects will often share valuable information such as children's names, vacation home locations, spouse's interests, etc., during these appointment setting phone calls and emails. Gathering information is important, but avoid long conversations about the campaign or projects—save that for the appointment.

Things to avoid:

- Don't talk to the spouse who has little or no interest in the organization.

- Don't call on Monday morning or Friday afternoon.

- Don't try to focus on other tasks when you need to be calling—set an allotted time each week for calling.

- Don't give away too much information.

- Don't use the term "meeting." It implies it will take a long time.

- Never mention money.

- Don't share information about the project costs or use the word "donate."

Helpful phrases:

- "Because of your past support…"

- "I understand you are busy, but we are very excited about the campaign and the opportunities this will provide…"

- "We would like to come and update you on what is happening at XYZ Organization…"

- "Visit with you", "Spend some time with you", "Share with you…"

Keys to Success:

- Staying organized is critical.

- Prepare accurate itineraries.

- Include appointment time, prospect name, location address, phone numbers, notes on parking and any special notes about the prospect.

You will get cancellations and no shows. But, one way to avoid this is to mail a reminder card a week before the booked appointment which gives the time, date and place that the appointment is slated with you. NO PHONE NUMBER is on the reminder card nor is there a request for a confirmation callback. The omission of a phone number is purposeful and is for the same reason we do not telephone to remind people of appointments. That would make it too easy for prospects to postpone, reschedule or even to cancel. In the event that they do postpone or cancel, immediately offer them other times or visits for the future while you have them on the phone. If a prospect does not show for a meeting, call them to confirm if they are running late or unable to attend and reschedule while you have them on the phone.

Setting appointments is the most difficult part of cultivation. Stay positive, be politely assertive, believe and support your mission, and keep calling!

CHALLENGE TO CHANGE

1. *Show a genuine interest in the person you are calling, as well as a support for your organization and its mission.*

2. *Mail a reminder card a week before the appointment, but don't include a phone number as that makes it easy for them to call and cancel.*

3. *Keep a mirror in front of you during your calls. Always smile!*

Psalm 19:14 "May these words of my mouth and this meditation of my heart be pleasing in your sight, Lord, my Rock and my Redeemer."

CHAPTER FOUR

THE CONTACT MEETING

The pre-qualification process is complete, and now you have a portfolio of contacts who are ready to be approached. There are four elements to this first contact meeting:

1. **Meet face-to-face:** I probably don't need to tell you this, but the most effective way to cultivate a donor is face-to-face. You can make phone calls, you can send notes or a newsletter, or you can stay in touch by email. While those are great tools, they are no substitute for the face-to-face visit. Further, try to always meet with the husband and wife together. Many times we meet with the man out of convenience, and he goes back and tries to communicate the meeting to his wife. A recent study shows that 90% of men indicate that the woman helps determine where and how much they give; thus, you need to include her too. If they cannot both be there for the preliminary meeting, ensure that both are included in the solicitation meeting.

Recently, I was told by an organization with which we were working that an individual had heard the executive director of the organization speak. He was very impressed with the work and impact the organization was making in changing lives. A few weeks later, he emailed the executive director to arrange a meeting. The executive director did not respond. The individual tried again with another email. This time, the email was passed along to the director of development who in turn responded and arranged a meeting with the individual. In doing research prior to the meeting, she discovered this individual and his wife had just won over $200 million in the lottery. The first meeting resulted in the couple giving the organization a check for $100,000, and a later meeting ended with an eight-figure pledge. Face-to-face meetings are important.

2. **Share information:** Is the purpose of the meeting to solicit? No, we're not ready for that. The purpose of the first meeting is to share information and try to determine their interest. At some point, you will have to ask them to contribute, and they are more likely to give if you ask for something they are interested in. Ask questions of the donor; get to know him or her, find out their interests; listen for clues that indicate interest in a particular aspect of your fund-raising project. Are you going to take notes in this meeting? No, because you don't want to lose eye contact with the donor.

Study the prospect's body language and learn to read his attitude. If his arms are folded and his legs are crossed, he may be feeling negative toward you or the project. It's not a very open meeting when someone is sitting in that position. If his body language changes during the course of the appointment, he may be feeling more inclined toward your project. Consider another scenario. I go into a meeting and the prospect is sitting behind his desk. He gets up and comes out from behind the desk, and he sits on a couch or chair beside me. Now, that's a much better meeting. Meetings where there is a desk as a barrier tend to be difficult. But, do I invite the prospect to come and sit on the couch? No. This is his office. Remember, you are a guest in the prospect's home or office.

A few years ago, I was training the development staff of a hospital in the Midwest. My training includes not only teaching proven methods in fund-raising, but also going on visits with individual development officers. I remember on one such visit, a preliminary meeting, the prospect invited us into his office. He sat behind his desk, and we sat in two chairs in front of the desk. As we sat down, the development officer immediately moved a stack of papers on the prospect's desk so he could place his materials on the desk. The meeting went well, but when we got back to the development officer's car, I told him he did two things wrong. One, you never move anything on the prospect's desk. Put your materials on the floor if you have to. And two, you were chewing gum! This development officer learned a valuable lesson and one he will probably never forget. We all make mistakes in this business, but it's how we learn from our mistakes that makes us better.

Back to the meeting. So, how do you know when to end the meeting? Body language offers clues. If the prospect suddenly changes positions in his or her chair, that's a strong indicator the meeting is over. If he is sitting back and leans forward, the meeting is over. If he's leaning forward and sits back, the meeting is over. Learn to read these signals because you don't want to over stay your welcome. I would rather have a 10-minute meeting of substance than a longer meeting with no substance at all.

3. **Go from general to specific:** The goal is to talk from general to specific about the organization and the current or pending capital campaign. When you do this, you are answering the question you know the prospect is asking: "Why have you come to see me in particular about this project?" Make the prospect feel good about the organization, where you're going and what you're doing. Talk in terms of people and benefits, not numbers. Talk about the impact your organization is having. Share specific information about the aspects of the upcoming campaign that you think is of greatest interest to the prospect.

The next page shows an example of a chart utilized by development officers at one of our athletic department clients.

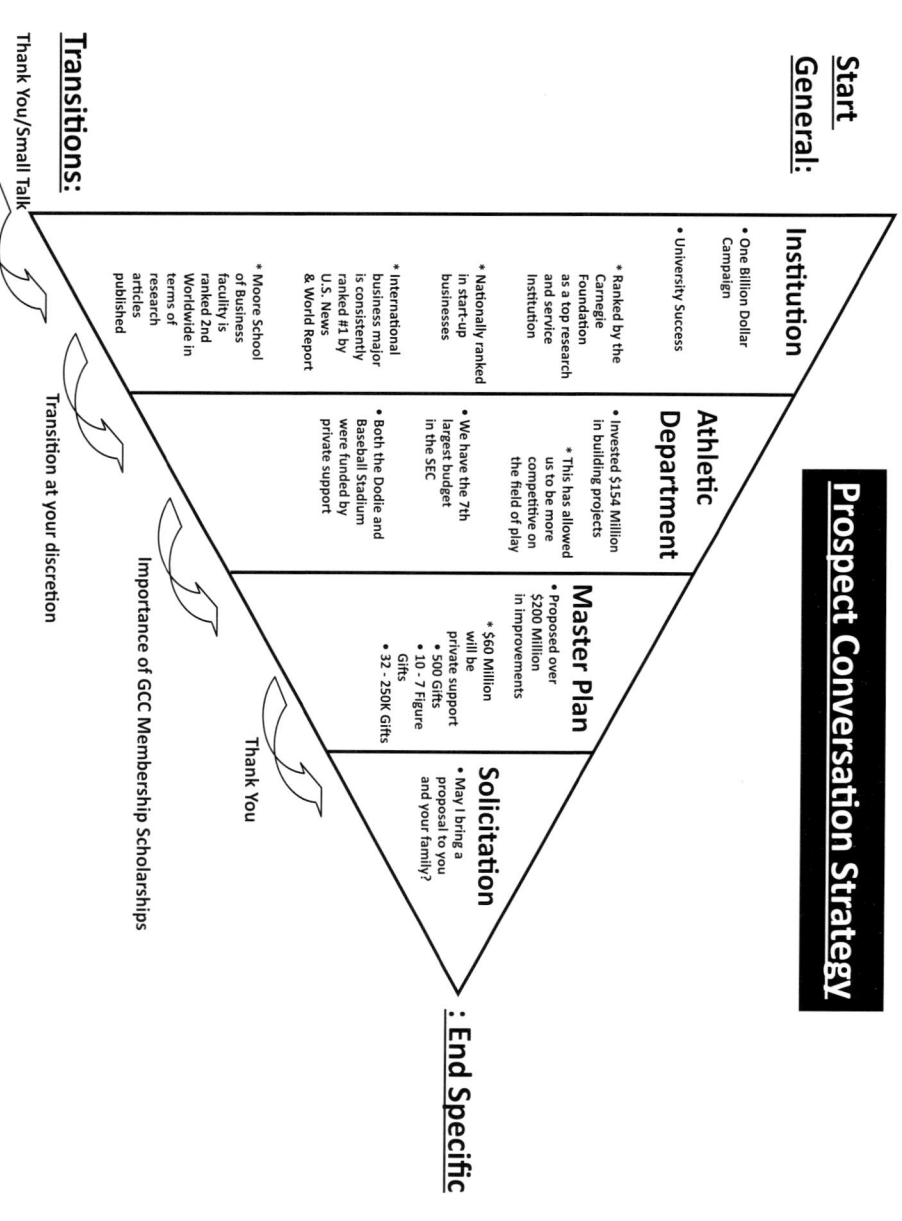

Prospect Conversation Strategy

Start
General:

Institution
- One Billion Dollar Campaign
- University Success
* Ranked by the Carnegie Foundation as a top research and service Institution
* Nationally ranked in start-up businesses
* International business major is consistently ranked #1 by U.S. News & World Report
* Moore School of Business faculty is ranked 2nd Worldwide in terms of research articles published

Athletic Department
- Invested $154 Million in building projects
  * This has allowed us to be more competitive on the field of play
- We have the 7th largest budget in the SEC
- Both the Dodie and Baseball Stadium were funded by private support

Master Plan
- Proposed over $200 Million in improvements
  * $60 Million will be private support
  - 500 Gifts
  - 10 - 7 Figure Gifts
  - 32 - 250K Gifts

Solicitation
- May I bring a proposal to you and your family?

: End Specific

Transitions:

Thank You/Small Talk

Transition at your discretion

Importance of GCC Membership Scholarships

Thank You

4. **Determine the contact's interest and inclination:** It's possible that the contact will interrupt you in the middle of your information sharing and say, "I really don't need any more information. I'm prepared to give toward this project." In over 34 years in this business, this has never been said to me. But, if it happens to you, it's a happy occurrence, but it doesn't signal the end of the meeting. Again, if you have done your homework, you will know his/her capacity to give. Once the prospect expresses a willingness to give, there is still the matter of "How much?" (See Section Three: Close). On the other hand, the prospect may share new information with you about his/her capacity to give of which you and your committee were unaware. This could be information that may remove this individual from your list of prospective donors altogether or may increase the ask amount.

You'll note that the four purposes of the first contact meeting say nothing about asking for money. I have left initial contact meetings with checks or signed pledge cards when a contact was eager to give. But that is the exception, not the rule. And that wasn't one of the purposes of the meeting.

Early in my career, I visited with a prospect to determine his interest in our campaign. He had just made a seven-figure gift to another institution in our area. Before I could get very far in my small talk, he gets up, walks to his desk and writes me a check for $25,000. Our organization wanted to bring him a proposal for a seven-figure gift, but he "cut me off at the pass" and gave me "go away" money.

On the other hand, it can take months or years for a contact to decide to make a major gift. If a contact doesn't voluntarily make a gift at the contact meeting, and you decide that they are a viable major gift prospect, you move to the second "C"—Cultivation. Cultivation is the bridge between the contact and the close.

Remember, a contact is an individual, company or foundation that has been pre-qualified as a prospective donor.

CHALLENGE TO CHANGE

1. *Always approach a prospective donor only after pre-qualifying his/her giving capability.*

2. *Strive to meet all four purposes when contacting a prospect: (1) face-to-face meeting where you (2) share information that is (3) tailored specifically for the contact that (4) prompts the contact to reveal his or her interest and inclination to give.*

"Success always comes when preparation meets opportunity."

Henry Hartman

CHAPTER FIVE

GIVERS GIVE

Albert Einstein's favorite saying was, "Not everything that counts can be counted, and not everything that can be counted, counts." That is true in fund-raising. Givers give for several reasons, but you have to remember---respect them and remember that manners matter.

One of the top reasons givers give is because they believe in the mission. One to two percent of the population give to presidential campaigns compared to about 70% of households that give to charity. Why? They believe in the mission of the organization.

People also give for emotional reasons. I recently saw a study where 28 gifts were sent to a number of hospitals. There were only a few warm thank you notes sent in return. Of those, some took weeks to arrive and one hospital took more than three months to respond. In another study, 100 organizations were contacted and asked how to join their annual giving program. Nearly half did not respond. If that is the standard, do you think donors will continue to give to those organizations or continue to call to ask how to give money? Probably not. Prompt thanking and returning phone calls is important. Remember to send thank you notes 48 to 72 hours after receiving the gift.

One way to thank donors is to take them on a site tour so they can see their dollars at work. Nothing is more powerful emotionally than seeing the impact of their dollars with their own eyes. Donors want to know and see how they are making a difference.

Booker T. Washington was raising money for Tuskegee Institute. John D.

Rockefeller sent a letter with $1. Washington sent a gracious thank you, and at the end of the fiscal year, he sent Rockefeller an exact accounting of what he had done with the dollar. There's no more critical trait for a fund-raiser than integrity. When people trust you, they are open to what you say, but trust takes time. You earn respect by showing that you genuinely care and that you are grateful.

Jon Huntsman, Sr., returned from a check-up with a bad diagnosis. He had prostate cancer. On the way to the hospital to begin treatment, he made three stops. First, he dropped by a homeless shelter and left a check for $1 million. Then, he stopped at a soup kitchen and handed over another check for $1 million. And finally, he dropped off a check for $500,000 at the clinic that had found the malignancy. He has always given more with his heart and less with his head. Of the 1,000 living billionaires in the world, he is one of 18 who have donated at least $1 billion. In 1960, as a Navy Lieutenant, he would take $50 out of his $320 monthly paycheck and give it to the Navy Relief Fund to help veterans' families. That was in addition to the $32 he gave to his church. Warren Buffet invited Huntsman to join him and others to sign a pledge of giving half of their money away. Huntsman said they had it all wrong—the right formula was to give 80% of it away.

Boone Pickens said, "I love making money, but I also love giving it away. Not as much as making it, but it's a close second." Pickens has given away close to $2 billion. His philanthropic approach has been, "I don't plant small trees. Why? Because of my age. I'm not out to change an organization for a day or a month. I'm out to change the lives of as many people as possible. I'm 80 years old. I want results now."

Again, there is no shortage of money—only a shortage of big, bold ideas. Fund-raising starts with passion. People want to give, even in tough times. Most people don't give to causes alone. They give to people who believe in causes. Know your mission, and no matter how you feel, get up, dress up and show up.

1. *Know your mission.*

2. *Communicate your organization's big bold ideas.*

Matthew 6:3-4 "But when you give to the needy, do not let your left hand know what your right hand is doing, so that your giving may be in secret. Then your Father, who sees what is done in secret, will reward you."

CULTIVATE

CHAPTER SIX

TODAY'S DONOR

I n today's world, the methods of fund-raising have increasingly become detailed processes with specific goals and measures. Professional fund-raisers continue to develop new techniques and skills to engage their constituency and raise more and more money for their organizations. The simplistic rules of asking for money by selling candy bars or generic direct mailings are becoming a thing of the past. By the same token, those who contribute to our organizations have evolved into a much more sophisticated constituency who **crave involvement, desire inspiration and require accountability.**

Donors Crave Involvement

A popular phrase used in fund-raising today is "dollars follow involvement." Involvement leads to commitment and commitment leads to dollars. Statistics show those who are involved in your organization give significantly more than those who do not take part in helping to fulfill your mission. The more you can involve volunteers in activities that bring them closer to your organization and the work you are doing, the more success you will have in fund-raising.

Why do volunteers volunteer?

- They believe in you the development officer.

- They are a board member.

- They want recognition.

- The most common reason they volunteer is because they believe in the mission.

How do you get volunteers involved?

- Invite them to your organization to see your day to day activities.

- Ask them to host an event and invite others to come and learn about your organization.

- Ask them to serve on an advisory committee or on your board of directors.

- Ask them to serve as the chair of a campaign or fund-raising initiative.

- Ask them to speak to your organization or board.

We recently conducted a campaign for a university's school of engineering. They developed a campaign committee named the Leadership Team which consisted of 14 members. The campaign raised over $100 million. The 14 members of the Leadership Team gave $39 million to the campaign. They were involved, they believed in the mission, and they were committed.

I once worked with an individual who was on the board of a bank in addition to serving on our client's board of directors. He had made a nice gift to our campaign. But, he did more than that. He also set up a meeting with the bank president to discuss a contribution to the campaign. He went with me, and we made the solicitation and got a six-figure gift from the bank president. He was capable of pulling that together because he had a relationship with the president and he was involved with the school.

Take for example a Christian school in North Carolina. The school had a parent who was a very prominent businesswoman with a great deal of affluence and capability to contribute to the school. While her line of work afforded her the financial situation to potentially give a large gift to the school, it also kept her extremely busy and unavailable to get very involved in the school. As a strategy to involve her despite her busy schedule, the school asked her to co-chair its capital campaign, which would allow the school to utilize her name and credibility to get others excited about the campaign. This allowed the busy mom to be involved on a level that she felt she could fulfill and at the same time maintain her busy work schedule. In the feasibility study, the woman gave the interviewer a range of $50,000 to $100,000 for her possible campaign gift. After being involved, her gift amounted to four times what she indicated in the study. This parent would have most likely given a gift to the school, but by involving her in the leadership of the campaign, the school was able to maximize her gift potential and received a sizably larger gift than originally expected.

An important point to remember when involving volunteers/donors is that you shouldn't rely on them to do all the work. You can't fire them, so choose them wisely. You want people who have the affluence to make a leadership gift and the influence to lead others to do the same. You don't just want good people. You want people who can make a leadership gift. Volunteers are used for two reasons. (1) They give more than a non-volunteer, and (2) they help duplicate the fund-raising effort. The goal of involving them is to give them a good experience where they invest time and energy into your organization, which will result in an investment of their money. Successful campaigns are staff driven, not volunteer driven. Volunteers are helpful and can open doors for the staff, but they will not make a campaign successful— the staff will.

Donors Desire Inspiration

When developing a case for support for fund-raising, we often think about all the things we need to fulfill our mission. Sometimes these needs can even include how much money we need to keep the lights on or the doors open. Donors today don't want to hear about what we need; rather, they want to be inspired to give by learning about how keeping the lights on or the doors open will impact your community. They are inspired by the opportunities their gift will provide, rather than the needs it will fulfill. It is important to be honest and clear about your desires, but focus on the outcomes that will result from contributions. Eliminate the word "need" from your vocabulary.

What are examples of opportunities vs. needs?

A new building

- Need: A new facility

- Opportunity: Increased space will enable your organization to serve more clients/students, therefore furthering your mission in your community.

New computers

- Need: New computers for administrative staff

- Opportunity: Improved efficiency and updated software will allow your administration to provide more services to more clients.

A non-profit organization in North Alabama made a presentation to a prospective donor about their opportunity to build a new facility. After they presented their case, the prospect sat back and said, "I'll think about it, but you haven't convinced me of the need. I don't care about buildings. What will happen if we don't do this?" The bottom line is that he wanted to know, "How many lives will this building save? Why do I care?"

The visit with the prospect was a wake-up call to leaders of the organization to remember to focus on the impact of the mission and less on the building and the money. The organization was able to restructure its presentation and proposal with the focus on the results and lives touched by their work, rather than the hard numbers and money needed. This shift in thinking resulted in significant progress made toward reaching their fund-raising goals and engaged more donors in what their contributions will accomplish.

Donors Require Accountability

Donors want to know how their gifts are being used and making an impact through your organization. This is not accomplished by sending them token gifts like refrigerator magnets, leather coasters or address labels in appreciation of their gift. It is imperative that your organization remain accountable to your donors and report back to them on how, why and where their money was spent. Share with them a specific person or program that was impacted because of their gift. This process often motivates the donor to give a second gift and, often times, an even larger gift to your organization.

How do you steward and show accountability?

- If they contributed to a campaign to buy new equipment, send them a picture of the new equipment in use, put a sticker on the equipment recognizing their gift, or invite them to see how the machine is making a difference at your organization.

- For people who contribute to a scholarship fund, have the recipient send a thank you note or set up a face-to-face meeting between the donor and the scholarship recipient.

- When someone contributes to an endowment, send a report of how the funds have performed in the market and what the interest earned will help provide for your organization.

A hospital in California conducted a campaign to purchase a new pediatric MRI machine. When the machine arrived at the hospital, it had to be lifted by crane to the pediatric unit on the top floor of the hospital. A development officer was able to capture the machine being delivered by taking a picture of the crane in action. She emailed the picture that day to the donors who helped purchase the machine with the simple heading, "The MRI machine is here because of you!" In response to the email, the hospital received several more donations from the donors who contributed to the MRI machine because of their excitement and gratitude for being able to see the results of their gifts.

CHALLENGE TO CHANGE

1. *Strategically involve volunteers in your organizations to bring them closer to your mission.*

2. *Develop your case for support in terms of opportunities not needs.*

3. *Provide stewardship reports to your donors that reflect how their gifts were put to work.*

"In order to succeed, your desire for success should be greater than your fear of failure."

Bill Cosby

CHAPTER SEVEN

TODAY'S DEVELOPMENT OFFICER

To be successful in this business of fund-raising, you cannot be afraid to make mistakes. All of us have made many mistakes—you just have to learn from them. A successful development officer must also learn to use his or her time wisely. If you want to raise money in today's society, you have to get out of the office and go see people. If you are sitting in your office, busy for eight hours a day, five days a week, you are busy but not productive. You are not affecting the bottom line. You can't wait for the knock on the door; if you do, you will be waiting a long time. And, if that knock does come, you will receive far less than what that donor is capable of giving. The general rule of thumb is that if someone gives a gift unsolicited, they are actually capable of giving five times that amount. So, you actually just cost your organization money by sitting at your desk waiting on the check.

People often ask me what to look for in a development officer. I truly believe development officers can be taught the fund-raising techniques, but they cannot be taught the natural talents and traits necessary in a successful officer. So, what are these talents and traits? Number one, an individual must believe in the mission of the organization. Know the mission statement and believe it. Development officers must believe in what they are selling. Number two, an individual must have good people skills. They must be able to communicate the organization's mission with verbal effectiveness. Speak with passion and enthusiasm in your voice; it's not what you say but how you say it. On the flip side, a development officer must be a good listener. Follow the 80/20 rule—listen 80% of the time and talk 20% of the time. Listen with your eyes. By paying close attention to people, you will learn even more than you needed to know. Number three, which I think is the most important, an individual must be detailed. Development officers must cross the T's and dot the I's. Do what you say sooner rather than later. Fund-raising is a detail business, so if a development officer lacks this key natural talent, I can assure you they won't last in this business. And number four, a development officer must have a strong work ethic. You have to be out there knocking on doors. Fund-raising is not a car lot---they are not coming to you.

Recently, while onsite with a client, I helped with interviews for a new development officer. The candidate I recommended had a pharmaceutical sales background. He didn't know fund-raising, but he had these four qualities. And, if he learns the strategies and techniques used in fund-raising, I think he will be a successful development officer.

There are no shortcuts in fund-raising. Development officers must be sincere and must look at prospects as friends. Every time you see a major donor, don't look at the dollar signs, but think about the friendships. Successful cultivation of a donor requires a sincere interest in building a friendship.

Development officers do not have to be extroverts to be successful. I've seen many outstanding development officers who were introverts. People who come from a successful sales background are not always successful in fund-raising. Good fund-raisers are hard to find today. In fact, I recommend to many organizations that they "grow their own" and look for the four qualities mentioned earlier.

1. *Get out of your office and go see people!*

2. *Remember to cross the T's and dot the I's.*

3. *View donors as friends and not as dollar signs.*

4. *Grow your own development officers.*

Colossians 3:23 "Whatever you do, do your work heartily, as for the Lord rather than for men."

CHAPTER EIGHT

GOLDEN KEYS TO CULTIVATION

The average American today contributes to 11 to 14 different charities each year. While that's the good news, the bad news is that often they don't know the good charities from the bad ones, and all of those charities are competing for dollars. Nor do they know how to put their charitable gifts to work in arenas that reflect their own passions and priorities.

That's where the art of cultivation comes in. In fund-raising, cultivation is the bridge between a potential donor and a gift that fulfills that donor's desire to reproduce him or herself— and his or her life and legacy.

While there are many aspects to cultivation in the field of fund-raising, see if you can find the key aspect in this definition:

Cultivation is the sincere desire on your part to build a *friendship*.

You have to like people to be a successful fund-raiser. And I mean *actually* like them, not pretend you like them in order to get a gift. Cultivation is often a long-term process, and most people can tell over time if they are being befriended in a superficial way, or whether they have met someone who is becoming a genuine friend—someone who cares about them *more* than they care about the gift they might give. If you have a tendency to use people to get what you want, to accomplish your agenda in life, I beg you not to continue in the fund-raising business. It's that kind of approach that turns people off and gives the entire industry a bad name.

Let me mention seven keys to cultivation that I have learned and implemented over the years.

1. **Be genuine:** Here's the #1 rule in fund-raising—Honesty is the currency of the kingdom. Think of all the ways it's possible to be dishonest when dealing with people in a fund-raising environment:

   - We can pretend to be someone we're not.

   - We can tell people what they want to hear instead of what they need to hear.

   - We can misrepresent the organization for which are raising funds.

   - We can feign friendship when money is the real goal.

   - We can make promises we know we can't keep.

   - We can make promises we can keep but fail to keep.

Honesty in relationships is like money in the market. It's a medium of exchange; it's how we do business. If we are dishonest, verbally or non-verbally, it's like going into the marketplace with counterfeit money. You're trying to give something that's worthless in order to gain something that has value.

I worked with a prospect whom we asked for a million dollar gift for an academic endowment. He came back to us and said, "For every game you play in my city, I'll donate $250,000 to the campaign." (The university was in a small town.) One thing you do not want is strings attached to any gift. We took that information back to the foundation's board, and the foundation board politely said, "Thank you but no thank you." He was clearly interested in something other than our mission.

Don't over promise and under deliver. If the donor asks for something or some information that you can provide, by all means, do what you say you will do. If you have control over it, and it is part of your mission, then do it. If you do not, make sure you say you will pass it along to the person in charge, and that person will get in touch.

What is exchanged in a fund-raising setting? Obviously, the organization receives money or other forms of value. But, in exchange, what does the donor receive? She should receive the complete confidence and satisfaction she has been led to believe she would receive from participating in the organization's present and future achievements. If the organization's identity, goals, values and potential have been misrepresented to the donor, then the donor has given something of value and received nothing of value in return. If that happens, that donor will be a one-time donor for sure.

2. **Follow the Golden Rule:** In other words, treat a contact exactly like you would want to be treated if the roles were reversed.

- Do you like to be pushed and pressured?

- Do you like to be manipulated?

- Do you like to be given only partial information?

- Do you like to be talked down to?

If you don't like those experiences then you can rest assured your prospects won't either. On the other hand, they will appreciate the exact opposite—being treated in a kind, courteous and respectful manner.

Why do you think a version of the Golden Rule is found in virtually every major religion of the world? Because it reflects human nature, and because it works! Put yourself in the place of your contacts. When you treat them the way you would like to be treated, you will win them as friends first and donors second.

3. **Go the extra mile:** I was working with a prospective donor who had become a friend. He was a board member of the organization for which I was raising funds. When his daughter got married, the ceremony was held in a very small church. I did not receive an invitation to the wedding, but I did receive an invitation to the reception. So I drove two hours to attend the reception. I spent 30 minutes at the reception, going through the receiving line, meeting the bride and groom and chatting with the bride's parents. And then I drove home. I invested nearly five hours in that event because he had become a friend who had invited me to a milestone in his family's life. This person became a major donor.

    Another friend of mine (also a donor and board member) fell ill at the time his board term expired and was hospitalized. It was traditional to present a gift to retiring board members, but this individual was unable to attend the reception to receive his gift. So I flew to South Georgia, drove to his hospital room and delivered the gift to him personally. I could have easily sent it by mail or a delivery service, but I knew it would mean more to him if it was delivered personally, along with the greetings and thanks for his service from the board. Long after that event, this gentleman always mentions this one act of going the extra mile.

    Do you appreciate it when people go the extra mile for you? Of course! When you do that for others, it conveys something special—and it will be remembered. If you go the extra mile, you will be miles ahead of your competition.

4. **Be thoughtful:** Once when I was employed by a university in their development office, the school's football team went to the Sugar Bowl for the first time. As part of the celebratory atmosphere surrounding those events, we were given watches commemorating the team's participation in the Sugar Bowl. It was a lovely and thoughtful memento of the occasion, but I immediately thought of someone who would cherish that watch even more than I would.

I was working with a contact who was a major gift prospect for the university and who was also a fanatic of the university's football team. I believed that the commemorative watch I had been given would mean a great deal to him, so I presented it to him as a gift.

Gift giving must be handled sensitively. There must be no hint of any *quid pro quo*. The recipient must know that the gift is "no strings attached"; that the basis of such a gift, or any act, is friendship, not the expectation of a gift in return. In the case of the friend to whom I presented the watch, there was a clear understanding so I did not hesitate to act.

In other words, treat potential donors the same way you (hopefully) treat your family and friends—with unconditional love and respect. What you do for them is done on the basis of unconditional friendship, not on the basis of any action expected in return. That said, once your relationship has been established on a friendship basis, thoughtful gestures and kindnesses can go a long way toward strengthening the bond between you and your potential donors.

5. **Keep your word:** Let's say you meet with a contact who is a highly organized, detailed individual. He is interested in your organization's mission, but he is also a thorough researcher. He asks if you could provide him with basic financial statements and annual reports for the organization's last five years of activity. You agree to gather that information and get it to him as soon as possible.

When you call him back a few weeks later to set up a second meeting, you hear this: "Well, I would be willing to meet again once I've looked at the financial statements and reports you said you would deliver to me. And to be honest, since I hadn't received those, I went ahead and committed the bulk of my financial giving for the year to some other causes."

Do what you say you are going to do, sooner rather than later. To be more specific, do it within 72 hours. Out of common courtesy at least, we should do what we say we are going to do. Remember, you may be the only link between a potential donor and the organization you represent. How you perform is going to color that person's perception of the organization as a whole. If you say you will do something but fail to follow through, how confident is that contact going to be about the organization using a designated gift for the purpose it was given? Will the organization follow through more faithfully than its representative?

Keeping your word applies to many areas of the fund-raiser's life (areas in which you have presented yourself as a professional):

- Be on time for appointments.

- Return phone calls promptly.

- Dress professionally and be well-groomed.

- Conform to your contact's culture. ("When in Rome…")

- Follow through on commitments and promises.

6. **Treat information as a sacred trust:** I have seen potential gifts lost as a result of a fund-raiser not treating a contact's personal information as a sacred trust. This should go without saying, but unfortunately it has to be stressed.

As mentioned before, information must be kept confidential and managed with the utmost integrity. Most institutions require confidentiality agreements with anyone with access to information, contact reports, names and giving records—not just staff, but also volunteers, board members, etc.

If you have the opportunity to call on wealthy potential donors, there is always the temptation to talk about their lifestyle to others. Don't! Nothing will violate your relationship—and a potential gift—with a prospect more quickly than his discovering that you have made him a subject of conversation to others. Information revealed to you in private should not go beyond the boundaries of your personal relationship.

The biblical concept of stewardship comes into play here. In ancient cultures, a steward was someone who was entrusted with the property of another to manage it in his stead—the closest modern example we have today might be a butler or nanny. It might be the management of money, of property, of information, or even of the rearing of children. When information is shared with you by a contact, you become a steward of that information. That is, you are expected to treat it *exactly* as the contact would himself.

I know of a development officer who met with a prospect, and in the course of the meeting the prospect shared that he had box seats at the Braves' games. The development officer remembered this, and a week later called the prospect to ask if he could borrow a couple of those tickets. I don't know about you, but I would not call and impose myself on a prospect in that way. It's not about you; it's about the prospect.

7. **Walk your talk:** You, and the organization you represent, must be above reproach. If either is not, you are in the wrong business. How well would your organization fare if the spotlight of public scrutiny were turned on it? People who have earned their money by honest, hard work are not likely to want to hand it over to those who don't do business the same way.

CHALLENGE TO CHANGE

1. *Always treat a prospective donor as you would like to be treated.*

2. *Go the extra mile and you will be miles ahead of your competition.*

3. *Build friendships with prospects.*

4. *Follow through with actions you've promised a prospective donor in a timely manner.*

"A successful man is one who can lay a firm foundation with the bricks others have thrown at him."

David Brinkley

CHAPTER NINE

TAPP YOUR WAY TO A GIFT

Let's think practically about the cultivation or preliminary meetings themselves. I like to call a cultivation meeting a preliminary or discovery meeting because you are there to learn and discover several things. In fact, you are there to discover four specific pieces of information. However, my experience has been (remember I've made all of the mistakes) that it may take you several meetings to learn all four. Don't worry, your chances of success when it comes time to close actually increase with the number of preliminary meetings you conduct. However, make sure that each meeting has an objective.

We're in the cultivation stage, you're meeting with your prospective donor and you're trying to determine the **four rights** before you move toward the close. I remember the four questions by using the word TAPP. I want to know the following:

- When is the right Time to make the solicitation presentation?

- What is the right Amount?

- What is the right Project?

- Who is the right Person to make the ask?

It might take you one meeting, two meetings, three meetings, or it may take you a number of meetings before you determine what those four rights are. But it's important that you answer these questions.

I'll tell you a story from a university client. We completed a feasibility study and moved into a capital campaign. We scheduled a preliminary meeting with a prospect who was interviewed in the study. My objective for this meeting was to answer all four TAPP questions. I said to the gentleman, "You indicated in the feasibility study you would consider accepting a proposal for the campaign." He said, "Yes," and I said, "I understand that you and your wife have an interest in the music building." Again, he answered, "Yes." "If we present a proposal to you for the music building, is that something you would consider?" He said absolutely; that would be his number one priority. I now know the project—the music building.

Next, I said, "In the study, you indicated a six-figure gift. Would you consider a seven-figure proposal?" He said immediately, "No, I don't think so." Then he said, "Well, maybe." He said go ahead and put the proposal together, and he would look at it, but he would probably not do a seven-figure gift. I now know more about the ask amount.

Next, I said that the university president had next Tuesday or Thursday open on his calendar, and asked the prospect if one of those days would be good to return for another visit. He said Tuesday would be fine. We set up the meeting with the president for 10 a.m.

What did I leave that meeting knowing? I have the time, next Tuesday at 10 a.m.; an amount, one million dollars; the project, the music building; and the person, the president. So I learned all four rights in one meeting. Keep in mind, getting all four objectives in one meeting does not always happen.

I'll tell you the end of the story. We go back, we make our presentation, and based on what he had told me in the preliminary meeting, I knew he would not agree to a proposal of a million dollars outright. Instead, we asked him to consider a pledge of one million dollars payable in an outright gift of $500,000 and a deferred gift of $500,000 in his estate plans. His eyes got big, he looked thoughtful for a moment, and he said, "Okay." He was 70 years old at the time, but had not thought about a deferred gift. He did the million dollar pledge. Now we certainly could have gone in and gotten an outright gift for a half million dollars, but we would have left a half million dollars on the table if we had not approached it that way.

In essence, cultivation reaffirms the time-tested message that, "It is more important to give than to receive." It means listening, it means waiting for the right time, and it means building a friendship. Whether a gift follows or not is up to forces beyond your control, but when you have done your part you will have made a friend you can keep—a relationship that may bear fruit at a time and in a way you least expect.

Remember, cultivation is the expression of your sincere desire to nurture an ongoing friendship that seeks to allow your contact to achieve his or her goals in life first and foremost.

CHALLENGE TO CHANGE

1. *Determine which TAPP question you want to learn the answer to before going to the preliminary meeting.*

2. *Brainstorm questions to ask the donor that will identify the answer to one of the TAPP questions.*

"Don't aim for success if you want it; just do what you love and believe in, and it will come naturally."

David Frost

CHAPTER TEN

THE BRIDGE TO THE NEXT MEETING

Sometimes I'm asked how it's possible to cultivate friendships with 150 to 200 prospects. You have to use a detailed, systematic approach. For years, I have used a contact report. Immediately after I leave my initial contact meeting with a potential donor, while the details of the meeting are fresh in my mind, I will fill out the contact report. In that report, I record *everything* I learned—what we talked about, what the contact himself stressed, what I learned about his life, vocation, family, pets, hobbies, background, goals, how he prefers to communicate (email? phone? other?), his interests, inclination, capacity to give, and his personal desires to make a difference in the world.

Over the last few years, I've been trying to get development officers to observe and listen to everything said in a preliminary meeting. I recently was on a visit with a development officer from a Midwestern university. The prospect was 72 years young, a graduate of the university and a retired pharmacist who had donated approximately $3,000 over the years, all to the School of Pharmacy. When we entered the house, the TV was on Fox News. I noticed a picture of John McCain and a statue of Ronald Reagan on the bookcase. We did not talk politics. We sat down to visit, and I noticed a copy of the Wall Street Journal and other financial magazines on the coffee table. We did not talk about the economy. Yet, I noted all these details.

The meeting went well, and when the development officer and I got back into the car, I asked him what he heard and what he observed. He listed about 25 things. Back at the university, we immediately listed our next steps. By observing everything, it is much easier to create a contact report. You never know what information you heard or observed that will be useful in the future. If development officers train themselves to mentally record everything they see and hear, they will be in a better position to determine the right ask amount and ask for the right project.

If you fill out a contact report and note 25 specific pieces of information about a contact, and you are responsible for 30 contacts, suddenly you've got 750 pieces of information to manage. Just wait until you call a donor's child by the wrong name, and you'll suddenly realize your need to get organized.

Words to the wise regarding contact reports:

1. Fill out your contact report immediately! Drive around the corner and pull over and record the information before you forget it. Or transcribe it into a small tape recorder as you drive away and fill out the report later. You'll be amazed how many details—especially names—you'll forget within an hour of leaving a contact meeting.

2. Don't record anything in a contact report you would be embarrassed for your contact to see. There have been court cases where a fund-raiser's contact reports have been subpoenaed and the information in them entered into public record. Be respectful and careful about what you put in writing.

3. Review your contact reports periodically. Remember my discussion of sightings earlier? If you run into a contact two weeks after your initial meeting, think how nice it would be to mention these personal items in the space of a five-minute conversation: "I recall that Robbie was trying out for quarterback on the high school team. How did that turn out?...I just read a great article on the *Sports Illustrated* web site profiling several NFL quarterbacks. I'll email the link to you and you could pass it on to Robbie if he's interested… Great to see you again—say 'Hi' to Barb for me." Get the picture? Nothing about fund-raising is mentioned. If you

review your contact reports on a regular basis, you will be prepared for those "divine encounters" that can make a difference.

4. Never take a contact report into a contact meeting—or a notepad. Listen with your eyes and ears. Don't take notes during the meeting. Remember, spend 80% of your time listening and only 20% talking. Learn to remember details and record them on your report after the meeting.

CHALLENGE TO CHANGE

1. *Listen with your eyes and ears. Mentally record all information during the meeting.*

2. *Store contact report information in your fund-raising data base as well as in hard copy form.*

3. *Review all reports before the next meeting with the prospect.*

Isaiah 41:10 "So do not fear, for I am with you; do not be dismayed, for I am your God. I will strengthen you and help you; I will uphold you with my righteous right hand."

CLOSE

CHAPTER ELEVEN

TIMING IS EVERYTHING

Whether you're baking a cake, playing the stock market, or proposing to your true love, timing is everything. This is especially true in fund-raising where there are no short cuts and nothing happens before its time. The longer I work in fund-raising, the more I realize that the timing of a gift is not something over which I have control. I can only control the timing of the ask and how much I ask a prospect to consider.

However, I've also learned there is a time to close.

A development officer I know once told me, "Jerry, I'm the queen of cultivation, but I just can't make the close." At least she knew what was lacking! Too many development officers are content to cultivate, cultivate, cultivate and never move toward the close.

Most people are familiar enough with professional sales terminology to know what is meant by "close." Anyone who has ever purchased a home has been to a "closing"—the meeting at which the deal gets done. Papers are signed, money is exchanged, and property changes hands.

In the fund-raising world, the close represents the same exchange that it does in the world of sales—information is shared, an agreement struck, a pledge or contract is made, and both parties leave satisfied that they are getting the best possible deal. In fund-raising, the contact has led to a period of cultivation that is characterized by discovery on both sides. The contact discovers whether the opportunity being presented is something that conforms to his desires, and the fund-raiser discovers the contact's capability and interest in giving. If things move in a positive direction on both sides, a close occurs.

See if you can identify the key word in this definition of a close—and figure out why it is the key to a successful close:

To close means to present a prospect with the opportunity to *give* a gift.

Occasionally in life, we receive gifts for which we have not asked. That even happens in the world of philanthropy. We occasionally read of a wealthy individual or couple who announces an unsolicited gift to a favorite charity or alma mater. Such gifts are usually sizeable, such as the huge gift Warren Buffett gave of the bulk of his billions to the Bill and Melinda Gates Foundation (around $30 billion, nearly doubling the assets of the Gates Foundation).

The receipt of such gifts does happen. But when it comes to fund-raising, the vast majority of money is received as a result of someone asking for it. And that is the highest hurdle for most fund-raisers to get over—looking a prospect in the eye and saying, "I would like to ask you and your family to consider a gift of $10,000 to the ABC school capital campaign, specifically targeted for the development of a reading and language laboratory."

It's the difficulty of asking that question that led my friend, the queen of cultivation, to tell me, "I get to be such good friends with my prospects that I feel bad asking them for money!" But she's not the only one with that problem. There are many "Queens and Kings of Cultivation" out there. They do not know when or how to close. Boone Pickens said, "Most fund-raisers aim, aim, aim, aim….they don't know when to pull the trigger!"

You begin to close and start working on getting an ask in front of them at your very first meeting. We worked with one organization—it was a university with a lot of prospects--and we set up the rule of three. The rule of three says you can have two preliminary meetings, but on the third meeting, you have to make a solicitation. Now, did we leave money on the table using the rule of three? Maybe in some cases we did. But, we felt it was important so that we could go see the multitude of prospects that universities have. If you are not out there soliciting, I will guarantee you one thing…you are not going to raise any money. You have to be out there asking people for money. That is what this business is about. The more you do this, the better you are going to get.

As stated before, there is a time for everything. A close could occur at the first contact meeting (if the prospect volunteers a gift—which happens rarely) or months or years after that first meeting. A financial gift takes on a life of its own. It grows and develops over time and reaches maturity at just the right time.

And sometimes a close happens in spite of, not because of, our efforts to bring it about. I recall the first close in which I participated—I went to ask a company for a gift of $250,000. I hardly remember a thing about the meeting because I was so nervous. I don't remember what I said or what they said. All I know is that when the meeting was over, they had agreed to give the gift.

There are three things I do remember about that close:

1. I asked for the gift.

2. A period of (seemingly interminable) silence.

3. The prospect said, "Yes."

We could have done without #2 (though it's a necessary part of the process), but I can tell you #3 would not have happened without #1. I had to ask for the gift—and that is the key, indispensable element of the close.

I often have fund-raisers ask me, "How do you know when it's time to close?" Obviously, some campaigns have an ending date, so your contact, cultivation and close must be completed by a certain date. But if the campaign has a targeted amount of money, rather than a calendar date, as its terminal point, you need other indicators to know when it's time to close—to ask for the gift.

CHALLENGE TO CHANGE

1. *Are there contacts in your portfolio that it is time to close? Analyze what is missing from the TAPP questions; if all are answered, schedule a closing appointment.*

2. *Don't be afraid to ask!*

Proverbs 16:3 "Commit to the Lord whatever you do, and he will establish your plans."

CHAPTER TWELVE

KEYS TO CLOSING

Closing can be fun. It means you've done all your homework, you have all the information you need, and you are ready to give a donor the opportunity to do something he or she is already inclined to do! So, why do we sometimes dread it?

I remember making three solicitation calls with the chairman of a campaign at a private school and the president and CEO of a major company in town. Prior to making the visits, I reviewed with the chairman our five steps to be used in that day's solicitations. After our third visit, we were headed back to the school, and he said to me, "Jerry, this was fun, but I can tell you that this morning before we started, I said to myself, 'I would rather have a root canal than ask someone for money.'" But, the steps we used that day, and that I use in every solicitation, made it an enjoyable outing for him.

Before proceeding to a close, here are five items that must be "checked off" by you and any others who will accompany you to the close:

1. Determine the "right" answers to the TAPP question (see the previous chapter).

2. Prepare a written, personalized proposal. The larger the gift you are asking for, the larger the likelihood that you may not get an answer at the meeting. Most people need time to review and consider what you have asked them to do—especially if it involves a significant financial commitment. The proposal is a document you can leave with the prospect containing the details of what you have asked.

A proposal is 50 percent appearance and 50 percent content. If it does not look good, they will not read it. I recommend a solicitation proposal of 10-15 pages; but, don't expect all prospects to read every page.

A proposal should include:

- A cover letter from the campaign chairman with the specific dollar ask amount included

- An executive summary of the organization briefly describing its history, mission and vision that is no more than two pages

- A project page describing the fund-raising opportunity

- A budget page outlining how the money will be used

- An invitation page restating the specific dollar ask; if a naming opportunity is included, it is stated on the invitation page ("In recognition of this gift, we will recommend to the board of directors that the music building be named in your honor.")

- Appendix with a list of board members, campaign donors (no dollar amounts), campaign volunteers, and copy of organization's 501 (c) 3 letter

3. Confirm the date, time and location of the meeting with all involved.

4. Review the donor's personal information. This especially applies if you are accompanied by organizational leaders who have not been intimately involved in the cultivation process.

5. Review the following five-step solicitation process with all who will attend the close from the organization. Make sure everyone knows what part they play in the process. Remember, everyone who goes on a solicitation has a role.

There are five steps to a successful solicitation that, when followed by the fund-raiser(s), will keep the meeting on track.

Step 1: Greeting, Introductions, Small Talk

If leaders of the organization are meeting the prospect for the first time, take enough time to establish familiarity. It is helpful to have those attending share their background and role in the organization. (Note: Keep a fair balance between the number of fund-raisers and prospects. If you are meeting with an individual or a couple, don't take a half-dozen people from the organization. Such an imbalance puts the prospects in a defensive posture. Having an equal number, or one more fund-raiser than the number of donors, is an acceptable balance.) You know the prospect(s). Talk to them about family, hobbies, occupation, items in their office or home, etc. It's an icebreaker for the prospect. This should be five to 10 minutes, but no more than 15.

Step 2: Summarize the Purpose of the Visit

If I'm a part of a solicitation, I always take this role. If not, the development officer should summarize the purpose of the visit as stated here:

"Bob and Ann, you and I have talked over recent weeks about your interest in supporting the campaign for XYZ College Prep Academy. We've prepared a proposal to leave with you for your consideration. We want you to read it, review it and consider it."

"But, for the next few minutes, I would like Dr. Martin, the head of XYZ, and John Foster, the board chairman, to share with you in greater detail the vision we have for this campaign and its potential benefits to XYZ students."

What does Step 2 accomplish? It tells them that I am not expecting an answer from them today. In this business, I'm trying to take pressure off of people, not put pressure on them. I don't want anyone to put pressure on me, so I'm taking pressure off of Bob and Ann. Also, I don't hand them the proposal until the end of the meeting. Why? Because I want them to listen to the head of the organization and the board chairman, not flip through a proposal. Don't put the proposal on the table or desk either, they may pick it up and begin reading it. Keep it in your hand until the right time to leave it with them.

Step 3: Tell the Story

If someone has accompanied you to the close (for example, "Dr. Martin" in Step 2), this is where he would present the vision for the project—going from general to specific. If you are presenting the proposal alone, you need to move forward with telling the story. I like to tell the headmaster, president or board chair, "Speak from the heart and be passionate." Concentrate on talking about people not numbers, and benefits not needs. While I don't suggest scripting this part, it is a good idea to review ahead of time with the headmaster, president or board chairman his or her thoughts and the main points he or she wants to cover. It's not what they say but how they say it. It's the passion and enthusiasm that will be remembered.

I learned not to put these bullet points in writing. At a university we prepared for a $5 million ask very carefully and created talking points for the president, athletic director and the head coach. They got to the meeting, which I did not attend, and as they were going through the process, the president pulled out his notes and looked them over to make sure he covered all of his points. That's when I stopped writing down the bullet points.

However, it is useful at this point to share 13x24 inch boards that depict campus renderings, building layouts, or whatever visual depictions will help convey the purpose of the project. Visuals are very helpful in telling the story.

Keep the story to 10-15 minutes. Then repeat a few bullet points, while continuing to be passionate and enthusiastic.

Step 4: The Ask

When the story portion is completed, I (or the development officer) should jump in and say,

"Bob and Ann, we have a proposal we're going to leave for you and we would like for you to review it and consider it. Let me tell you where we are in the campaign right now."

I believe the development officer should be making the ask, not the headmaster, president or board chair. The reason I believe that is because whoever makes the ask should be following up. I don't think the headmaster, president or board chair will be the one to follow up. That is the development officer's role.

I (or the development officer) tell the prospect what has been raised to date in gifts and pledges, and I also mention that the board of directors is 100% in commitment as well as the staff. I want to show them that the campaign is successful and the board and staff are committed to the project too. Then, I make the ask for a specific dollar amount.

"Bob and Ann, we would like for you to consider a gift of $15,000, payable in equal amounts of $5,000 per year over the next three years in support of the campaign."

Silence. Once the ask is complete, let the prospect(s) be the next person(s) to speak. The biggest mistake development officers make is they don't stop talking. They keep going. This is the silent phase. We are waiting on the response.

You can expect one of three responses: Yes, no, or we will consider that. If you've done your homework, you should not receive an outright rejection. Ninety percent of the time, the response is a statement along the lines of, "We will think about it." After their response, always say, "Any amount you give will be greatly appreciated." Once again, you are taking the pressure off.

Step 5: Follow-up

The final step in the close is to ask permission to follow up with the prospect in a week to 10 days.

I (or the development officer) will ask:

"Bob and Ann, with your permission, may I call you in a week or so to follow-up— to see if you have any comments, questions or concerns about the proposal?"

The answer is almost always "Yes," and the donor often volunteers information about the best time or specific date to call. Now you give them the proposal.

Now, sometimes you have to think quickly on your feet and may not even give them the proposal. I made a solicitation in Texas with the president of an organization. We had a proposal we were making to an older gentleman with an ask amount of $35,000. I had the proposal in my hands, we went in, sat down, and on the conference table in his office was an envelope. He slid it over to the president and said, "Here is my commitment." This was before we could even get into any small talk. The president opened the envelope and there was a check for $25,000 and a pledge for $250,000. Remember, our proposal amount was $35,000. Do you think I gave him our proposal? Absolutely not! When we left, the proposal left with me.

CHALLENGE TO CHANGE

1. *Avoid asking the question, "How's business?" during small talk.*

2. *Always come to the solicitation with a written proposal that can be left with the prospect.*

3. *After making the ask, always let the donor speak first. Silence is not a bad sign!*

4. *Ask permission to follow up.*

"I don't measure a man's success by how high he climbs, but how high he bounces when he hits bottom."

George S. Patton

CHAPTER THIRTEEN

THE ASK

When making the ask during a solicitation visit, it is imperative to always ask for a specific dollar amount. I have found that if you don't, you end up leaving money on the table…and usually a significant amount. The _biggest mistake_ _made in fund-raising today is not asking for a specific dollar amount._ There is one sentence that you must remember to use: "Will you consider supporting (Organization Name) with a gift of $$ payable in equal amounts of $$ per year over the next three to five years?"

You can see from the statement above that I always break up the payment in equal amounts and verbally spell that out for the prospect. One time I was on a solicitation visit during which we asked a woman for $18,000. She considered it and told us that amount was just too much. Yet, when we broke it down for her, showing it was $6,000 per year, she changed her mind and made the pledge.

But be careful, I do think you can ask for too much. Don't ask someone for $1,000 when you know they can only give $100, and don't ask someone for $100 when you know they can give $1,000. If you ask for $15,000 and they say they can only commit to $10,000, then take it. Ask if they would be willing to sign a pledge card, pull it out of your pocket, get it signed and move on. If they are not comfortable signing a pledge card today, ask if you can follow up in a couple of weeks, and do it. My mother taught me a bird in the hand is worth more than two in the bush. Take it and move on.

It is easy to think you've made yourself clear when you have not, so be sure to ask directly for a pledge, and be positive about it. When asking for a specific amount, use such phrases as support, pledge, gift and investment.

Avoid words like money and donation. And after the ask, always be sure to wait for their response. Don't take the ask back before they've had an opportunity to consider it. A moment of silence is not negative.

To illustrate the importance of asking for a specific dollar amount, consider the following experience:

We were working with a school on a campaign. The chairman of the campaign and I were going to solicit some grandparents. We had a proposal in hand for $50,000. We walked in, sat down and started with small talk. The gentleman said they had been following the campaign and were impressed with the way it was going. He went on to say that they were ready to make a pledge of $500 to the campaign. The chairman of the campaign started to get up, but I intervened and said, "We do appreciate that and thank you, but that's not the dollar amount we have in the proposal." The woman then asked what that amount was. Instead of an immediate answer, I went right back into step number two of the solicitation and walked through the presentation. Then, when the time came, I asked them for $50,000.

They didn't end up doing $50,000, but they did pledge $15,000. That's a long way from $500. So again, always ask for a specific dollar amount so you don't leave money on the table.

CHALLENGE TO CHANGE

1. *Always ask for a specific dollar amount in a solicitation.*

2. *Break out the gift amount in equal payments over a three to five year period.*

Philippians 4:13 "I can do all this through Him who gives me strength."

CHAPTER FOURTEEN

THE FOLLOW-UP

S ometimes I am the one to make follow-up phone calls to prospects. If I'm on the phone calling Bob and Ann, I'm not going to say to Bob when he answers, "Hey Bob, have you made up your mind yet? Do you have a decision on that proposal?"

Instead, I am going to be politely assertive and say something like this:

"Bob, this is Jerry Smith. I wanted to call and follow up on the proposal presentation that Dr. Martin and I made to you last week. I just wanted to see if you had any comments, concerns or questions about the proposal."

Typically, there's a reply like this: *"No Jerry, we haven't really looked at the proposal,"* or, *"Yes we're looking at it now. We're reviewing and thinking about it."*

Then what I would say is, *"Bob, is it okay if I call you back in a week?"* Always ask permission to follow up, give a time to follow up, and do it.

In all my years of fund-raising, I've had very few prospects say, "No," to a proposal. Usually, they will either give what they've been asked to consider, or they will give a lower amount. But, occasionally I've been told, "Jerry, we are just not going to be able to do that."

At that point, I use the four IPAT questions created by Jerry Panas, philanthropy consultant. The only way to continue to cultivate this donor is to try and understand why they are declining to give. Here's how the IPAT questions work:

"Bob, may I ask you a question?" (I don't say, "Bob, may I ask you four questions?")

"Is it the **institution** or the organization—is that why you have not committed to the campaign?"

"No. That's not it."

"Is it the **project,** because I thought that was the project you were interested in?"

"No. The project's fine. I really like the project. That's the project that I would probably support if I were going to make a pledge."

"Well, is it the **amount** of money that we asked you to consider?"

"No, Jerry it's not. That's probably what we would think about giving."

"So, Bob, is it the **timing?**"

"Yes it is. We have three other pledges that we're trying to make. We're trying to complete those pledges, and we have a year and a half left to be able to do that."

"Bob, this is a five-year campaign. Would you consider making a pledge today and not starting your pledge payments for eighteen months?"

"I can do that."

This conversation actually happened to Jerry Panas, and it is the scenario that convinced me again of the importance of asking questions. He was able to close on a $100,000 gift simply by asking questions.

Give them a sense of urgency. Why is it important for them to commit now instead of next week, next month or next year? A sense of urgency can motivate them to make a commitment today.

Some examples are:

- We can't break ground until we have $__.

- We have a matching opportunity and that opportunity is only good for ____period of time.

- We are $__ away from our goal and would like for you to make the gift that puts us over the top.

- We'd really like to acknowledge your gift in the next newsletter, at the next event, etc.

A close has occurred when you leave with or receive a signed pledge card. I don't like to leave the pledge card with the prospect because it takes away one of the reasons for my follow up. A pledge card in the mail is like a check in the mail. It never gets there. I am willing, however, to take a pledge over the phone with the prospect's permission, and I make a note on the pledge card that it was received by phone, on this date, by me, and I sign the card. The acknowledgement letter mailed to the donor from the organization should state the pledge was received by phone and restate the amount and payment schedule so the donor can be sure it was received correctly by the organization.

Colin Powell's Rules for Success apply to our industry too:

- It can be done.

- Check the small things.

- Share credit.

- Remain calm.

- Be kind.

- Have a vision.

- Be demanding.

- Perpetual optimism is a force multiplier.

Remember, to close means to present a prospect with the opportunity to give a gift. Once you close on a gift, you're not finished. The next steps of gift acknowledgement and stewardship lead to further cultivation, which leads to future gifts. The cycle of contacting, cultivating and closing are repeated day after day and week after week in the life of the fund-raiser—they are the three C's that lead to success!

CHALLENGE TO CHANGE

1. *If a prospect is hesitant to make a gift, use IPAT to determine why.*

2. *Give the prospect a sense of urgency to give to your organization.*

"The difference between a successful person and others is not a lack of strength, not a lack of knowledge, but rather a lack of will."

Vince Lombardi

CHAPTER FIFTEEN

THANK YOU

Saying "thank you" is the most important phrase you can learn as a fund-raiser. Nothing, and I mean nothing, means more than a sincere thank you. I received the following email from one of our client's executive directors (forwarded from a donor), which illustrates my point well.

> *I received your thank-you letter with personal note for the Boston butt from Jimmy. I really didn't expect a thank-you, because the Boston butt has value (which we'll enjoy on the 4th!).*

> *I wanted to share this contrast: I made a $100 donation in early April to another nonprofit in honor of a prominent local businessman who I'd previously served with on a board. The check was cashed immediately, but I never received acknowledgement--either from the organization or (more importantly) from the honoree. I called the nonprofit and was told that they only acknowledge gifts of $250 or more, because that's all that's required by the IRS. I'm left to wonder if the person I was honoring even knows I made a gift to honor him.*

> *No wonder your organization weathered the recession so well..... Jerry Smith's formula works. And if I'm fortunate to work in the nonprofit arena again, it's an example I won't forget!*

The "thank you" is the final and most important step to close a gift. If you do not steward the donor properly after they make a gift, the chances of them giving again are slim to none. Standard practices should be in place for your organization to ensure that all donors are thanked and thanked in a timely manner—within 48 hours. Gifts are not just cash in hand. You should also have standards in place to thank donors for planned gifts such as bequests or life insurance; pledges to be paid over multiple years; gifts of stock; and gifts-in-kind. One person should be responsible for implementing standard practices whether you have a small donor relations office with one person or a large staff of 20. Someone has to be accountable for thanking donors and continuously stewarding them.

The donor must be thanked a minimum of seven times in seven different ways before asking for another gift. This starts with the detailed and personalized gift acknowledgement letter. Below are other ways to say "thank you":

- If a donor stops by your office or organization, always allow time to meet with them even if they didn't have an appointment, and always thank them for coming by.

- If a donor contacts you with a question or asks a question in an appointment, get them the answer quickly—the right answer—don't make one up, and thank them for contacting you.

- Establish special giving societies and/or host receptions or events to thank members.

- Send an email blast to all donors thanking them for their gifts. Include a current link to your website, an update on the projects they have supported, and a very short, to the point message.

- A donor wall can influence someone's decision to give, and it serves as a great way to recognize and thank donors. When donors make a gift, always ask how they would like their names to be listed when they are recognized: Mr. and Mrs. John Doe; Mr. John Doe; Mr. John Doe and Mrs. Jane Doe, etc. If you ask, do it correctly!

- A handwritten note is the best way to convey sincerity. It takes time to write and mail a personal note, and that's why it means more than other forms of communication like phone calls, emails, publications and form letters.

- Follow through with dedications and naming opportunity recognition events. It's important to thank the donor publicly when the project is complete with a reception or event of celebration.

- Send your donors birthday and holiday cards.

- Select mementos specific to different levels of giving that are meaningful to your organization.

There is a perception that organizations don't spend donated funds in the manner they were intended—you can fix this with GOOD COMMUNICATION! Donors need to be assured their gifts will be used for the purposes for which they were given. Below are a few tips to ensure effective communication with donors:

- Put gift acknowledgment policies in writing. As mentioned before, an acknowledgment should go out within 48 hours of receiving the gift. The acknowledgement should be personalized and include a specific description of the designation so that the donor knows you put their money where they want it to be used.

- Ensure that every donor is thanked no matter the size of the gift. There may be different letters or cards for different levels of giving, but some type of acknowledgement should go out for every level. Those $5 donors today could be your major gift donors of the future—if they trust you to use their money wisely.

- Regularly include donor gift profiles in each issue of your constituency newsletter or magazine. This is a great way to publicly recognize the generosity of major donors and serves to plant the seeds of philanthropy in others' minds.

- Always emphasize the impact of the gift as well as the donor and amount when you release publications. Donors want to know how their gift has made a difference. Donors are inspired by the opportunities their gift will provide—not just the need it will fulfill.

- If you have a donor wall, be sure that all marketing efforts state that anyone who gives above a certain level will have their names listed on a donor wall for permanent display, and make sure everyone's name is there and listed correctly.

- Set a standard for dedications for naming opportunities. It's important for all donors to be timely recognized and recognized equally among their peer donors.

- Keep donors up to date on their endowments and how they are being used with quarterly or annual reports.

To be a good steward, you need to be organized and track how and when donors are thanked. One way is a simple Excel spreadsheet with the donor's name, details, contact information, last contact date and type, and when the next contact and type should be made. Another way is to put together a donor matrix that is very specific with what type of communication and stewarding each level of donor receives. Track donors based on their level of giving to make sure everyone at every level receives every method of stewarding your organization has defined. Perhaps annual giving donors of $1,000 or less receive an acknowledgement letter from the annual giving director; donors of $1,000 to $4,999 receive a letter from the dean, vice president of development or headmaster; donors above $5,000 receive letters and a spotlight in the monthly e-newsletter, etc. This matrix will be different for each organization based on meaningful gift levels and your abilities to steward.

The following chart depicts what I like to call the lifecycle of a continuous donor.

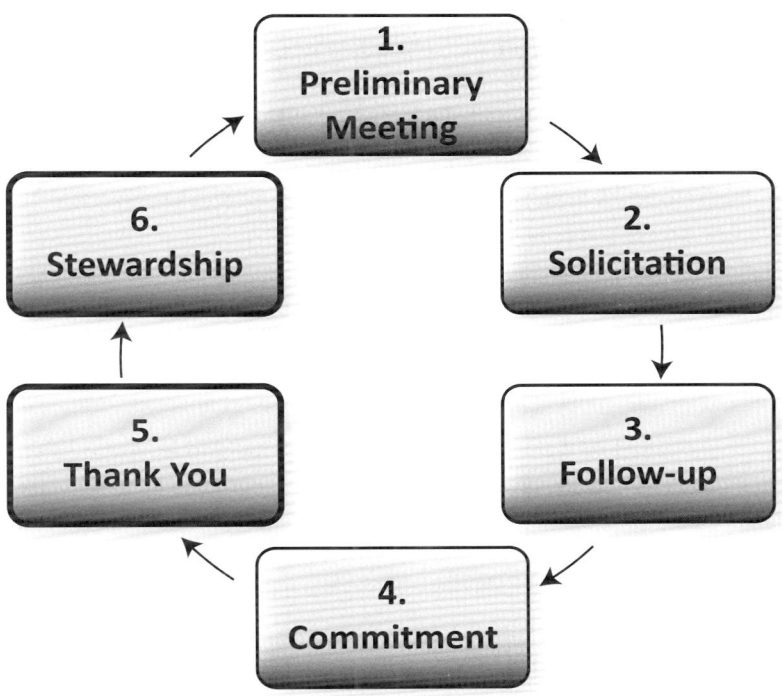

Never underestimate the value of strong donor relations and stewardship. This is the last step of closing the gift, but it is also the first step in soliciting the next one. The "thank you" is vital to the success and the future of your organization!

CHALLENGE TO CHANGE

1. *Always thank a donor a minimum of seven times in seven different ways before asking for another gift.*

2. *Assure donors their gifts are being used as they requested with effective communication.*

3. *Organization is key. Track how and when donors are thanked.*

Colossians 3:17 "And whatever you do, whether in word or deed, do it all in the name of the Lord Jesus, giving thanks to God the Father through him."

CHALLENGE TO CHANGE

1. *The names in your portfolio of prospective donors should be pre-qualified.*

2. *Spend your time building relationships with pre-qualified contacts.*

3. *Consider using electronic screening, especially if your data base is large.*

4. *Use both objective and subjective information in determining the right ask amount.*

5. *Show a genuine interest in the person you are calling, as well as a support for your organization and its mission.*

6. *Mail a reminder card a week before the appointment, but don't include a phone number as that makes it easy for them to call and cancel.*

7. *Keep a mirror in front of you during your calls. Always smile!*

8. *Always approach a prospective donor only after pre-qualifying his/her giving capability.*

9. *Strive to meet all four purposes when contacting a prospect: (1) face-to-face meeting where you (2) share information that is (3) tailored specifically for the contact that (4) prompts the contact to reveal his or her interest and inclination to give.*

10. *Know your mission.*

11. *Communicate your organization's big bold ideas.*

12. *Strategically involve volunteers in your organizations to bring them closer to your mission.*

13. *Develop your case for support in terms of opportunities <u>not</u> needs.*

14. *Provide stewardship reports to your donors that reflect how their gifts were put to work.*

15. *Get out of your office and go see people!*

16. *Remember to cross the T's and dot the I's.*

17. *View donors as friends and not as dollar signs.*

18. *Grow your own development officers.*

19. *Always treat a prospective donor as you would like to be treated.*

20. *Go the extra mile and you will be miles ahead of your competition.*

21. *Build friendships with prospects.*

22. *Follow through with actions you've promised a prospective donor in a timely manner.*

23. *Determine which TAPP question you want to learn the answer to before going to the preliminary meeting.*

24. *Brainstorm questions to ask the donor that will identify the answer to one of the TAPP questions.*

25. *Listen with your eyes and ears. Mentally record all information during the meeting.*

26. *Store contact report information in your fund-raising data base as well as in hard copy form.*

27. *Review all reports before the next meeting with the prospect.*

28. *Are there contacts in your portfolio that it is time to close? Analyze what is missing from the TAPP questions; if all are answered, schedule a closing appointment.*

29. *Don't be afraid to ask!*

30. *Avoid asking the question, "How's business?" during small talk.*

31. *Always come to the solicitation with a written proposal that can be left with the prospect.*

32. *After making the ask, always let the donor speak first. Silence is not a bad sign!*

33. *Ask permission to follow up.*

34. *Always ask for a specific dollar amount in a solicitation.*

35. *Break out the gift amount in equal payments over a three to five year period.*

36. *If a prospect is hesitant to make a gift, use IPAT to determine why.*

37. *Give the prospect a sense of urgency to give to your organization.*

38. *Always thank a donor a minimum of seven times in seven different ways before asking for another gift.*

39. *Assure donors their gifts are being used as they requested with effective communication.*

40. *Organization is key. Track how and when donors are thanked.*

ABOUT JERRY F. SMITH
AND THE J.F. SMITH GROUP

"One thing I've learned is that institutions, over time, become the extended shadow of their leader. Jerry F. Smith is the consummate professional in fund-raising. He has many, many years of experience, and he's learned a lot of valuable lessons that make him, and his organization, the best there is."

-- Jerry Reeder, Headmaster, Whitesburg Christian Academy

"Jerry Smith is the quintessential resource for fund raising... and for approaching life with gusto. His mentoring, his ability to connect with any audience, and his "never give up" approach to hard tasks gave me all the tools I needed to tackle a building program that sane people told me was "impossible for a small non-profit center." With Jerry's wise guidance and God's grace, we made history. Daunting obstacles are exciting challenges to Jerry. He throws his whole life into each one, forging on with a smile as he pulls the rest of us along with him."

-- Austin Boyd, Building Committee Chairman, Choose Life of North Alabama

"Your session at last week's conference was one of my highlights of the week. I learned so much that I think my hand nearly fell off from writing notes so frantically! It's not so much what you said, but it was how you said it and in what order. Just to hear your thought process was beneficial. What a treat it was for me to attend your session! It exceeded my expectations."

-- Alissa Campbell Shaw, Sr. Advisor, National Marketing Director,
ALSAC/St. Jude Children's Research Hospital

"It is uncommon today to find an organization that conducts business with the integrity and professionalism that has been demonstrated by all associates of the J.F. Smith Group. Their leadership, encouragement, and creative ideas are unparalleled in the industry. The guidance provided by Jerry Smith and his associates has been invaluable in helping us meet our development goals."

-- *Susan Coulter, Former Vice President of Advancement, University of Texas Health Science Center at Houston*

"Jerry Smith's guidance and leadership were certainly major reasons we were able to attain such remarkable results. He has done so much for our college, and I will never be able to express my gratitude for all his efforts on our behalf. Now we are on the verge of achieving what, five years ago, most thought was impossible."

-- *Larry Benefield, Former Dean, Auburn University College of Engineering*

"Your contribution as a speaker helped to make this year's conference an outstanding educational experience for our participants. The excellent presentations from talented people like you are what made it possible for the overall event to earn such positive feedback from those who attended."

-- *Tai Conley, Programs Services Specialist, Education & Training, 2013 AFP International Conference*

"Jerry and his staff were with us every step of the way during our recent campaign. Their expertise and counsel guided us in setting sensible campaign goals; and their credibility and confidence were reassuring as we moved forward together through a most difficult economic climate. The J.F. Smith Group delivered for Jesuit Dallas."

-- Chuck Vinson, Vice President of Institutional Advancement,
Jesuit College Preparatory School of Dallas

"The J.F. Smith Group associates were sincerely interested and enthusiastic in their support of our campaign. They provided me and my staff with an enormous educational experience through their expert guidance, advice and very active engagement. They took the time to really understand our institution, our unique mission and our needs and tailored a campaign that is providing the best opportunity for success. As a group, they are creative, flexible and a real pleasure to work with. In my opinion, their level of expertise, years of experience, work ethic and highly personable approach make them the best in their field."

-- Suzanne McKee, Vice President for Institutional Advancement,
Marion Military Institute

"When we worked with the Smith Group for our capital campaign, Jerry always kept our staff focused on the job at hand. He did not let us veer away from our mission to raise money for the university. I am very pleased that Jacksonville State University chose to work with the J.F. Smith Group in our fund-raising efforts. We would make the same decision again."

-- Dr. William Meehan, President, Jacksonville State University